STORIES OF FAITH ON THE JOURNEY TO GOD

JOANNE MCKENNA

ISBN
978-1-959314-28-8 (Paperback)
978-1-959314-29-5 (eBook)

Dedication

This book is dedicated to spiritual seekers
everywhere on a journey to God.

TABLE OF CONTENTS

Acknowledgments

No book is ever the product of one person's efforts, and this one is certainly no different. For myself, I am indebted to my family and friends, who are the moral fiber behind these pages; especially my parents who passed on their faith, dedication to family values, and unconditional love. I am grateful to my husband, James, for his constant love and support without which this would not be possible. To his sons, Todd and Kyle and the entire McKenna family, to my daughter, Melissa and my grandchildren Justice, Alyssa, Zion and Zachai; I am so very proud of them all.

I am eternally grateful as well to my wonderful sisters and their families; Sandra, Patty and Timi-Ann who exemplify the true meaning of family. I am especially grateful to our sister Audrey for her generosity and support while battling cancer with incomparable courage. I would like to thank my nieces and nephews; especially Elizabeth Ferri, for her research assistance.

I am indebted to Paula Hillman for her generous gift of time, and her trust in the triune God.

"Give thanks to God, bless his name; good indeed is the lord, whose love endures, whose faithfulness lasts through every age" (Psalm 100 : 4–5)

Prologue

Spiritual seekers around the world each have a story. It is our stories that accumulate and give basis to the evolution of a call and a choice. This is one faith journey of prayer and meditation. Each chapter begins with a story that impacted the choice which led to a deepening of love and longing for God. It is the revelation of the breadth and the depth of his love for us, the endless mercy which allows us to begin again and again, reminding us that he is with us... always.

This book is comprised of essays and prayers which tell the story that gave way to countless shattered constructs and the evolution of unknowing.

Its chapters are artificially divided as if linear. Recognizing that the spiritual life obeys no such order, one is imposed for the sake of deference to a process inherent in any meaningful relationship:

Beginning; with a story giving birth to
Choosing a path which develops into a
Longing and depth of
Loving which demands vulnerability,
Reconciling, before sight is restored and
Awakening becomes possible.

Preface

"The glory of God is man fully alive," said Iraneus.[1] What does it mean to be "fully alive" and how does it manifest God's glory? These questions marked the beginning of a deliberate journey more than fifty years ago. Since then, my longing to proclaim my own profound fiat has led to a progressive renunciation, a "via negativa" as it were.[2] This journey in search of at-one-ment or no-self has indeed been one of endless humility. Unlike anything I could ever expect or imagine, the nature of his glory continues to unfold.

"Make use of a method when you need it and as you pray... you will discover the wide horizon of each prayer," says *Rule for a New Brother*.[3]

Ambrose, fourth century bishop of Milan, said, "All that is true, by whomever it has been said, is from the Holy Spirit."[4]

While I have always been, and continue to be a practicing Catholic, my search for God has included an amazing adventure into Buddhism. I had always enjoyed silence and was drawn to contemplative spirituality. My introduction to Eastern spirituality began while on a monastic retreat at a Benedictine monastery led by a Jesuit priest. The retreat was a mix of Lectio, contemplative prayer and meditation based on the Buddhist tradition of Insight Meditation or Vipassana.

Assumption: Union with the living God and no-self are not even remotely related.

> Questions: Is there more congruence between contemplative spirituality and Buddhist psychology than is otherwise apparent? One naturally fosters the growth and practice of the other. True or false? Christianity is a highly-personalized religion, and Buddhism advocates self-annihilation; how can there be common ground, I asked along with countless inquirers of the East-West traditions.

It is in the depths of one's **own** heart, says Don Juan that such things are learned, and it is out of the depths of my own heart that I now share my experience of the common ground in search of glory.[5]

BEGINNING

Firsts—Live or Die

What is it about firsts that hits me square in the chest with pangs of fear? Is it the unknown? Is it the imagination? Is it the sense of powerlessness or the fear of failure? What stops me dead in my tracks at the threshold of nearly every beginning I can recall?

Dead is an interesting word to use in the context of first, but fear, like a vector of impending doom, seems to threaten the life of all that is familiar, concrete, in control, and successful. I didn't know this standing at the threshold of first grade. I hadn't even grasped it by twenty-six on my first visit to the

Buddhist monastery; two firsts that had a lot more in common than readily apparent.

Windmill Street School was a massive showcase of adjoining brick buildings. It extended beyond an entire corner block. Its incline required the immense concrete staircase to rise to an unimaginable three levels. A sweeping cement banister bordered this one hundred-year old masterpiece. Its height generously exceeding my own was wide enough to accommodate the bottom of a moderately sized child. Iced with pink and beige marble, it looked more like a waterslide than a balustrade.

At six, I stood at the base of this stone monster gazing in awe at the three distinct landings exposing angled entries. The metal doors, newly painted, reflected strategically placed teachers nearly transfigured by the early morning light. There was nothing at all familiar about this vantage point. It may well have been at a new school in a different town because, as kindergartners, the street lined entrance was off-limits.

How would I negotiate the immense risers? What if I tripped? Undoubtedly, those slippery chunks on either side did not offer any reassurance whatsoever. After all, it was not so long ago that I traded metal braces for leather-laced boots. They were equally ugly but less noticeable to support my clumsy legs. Even if I did reach the safety of a landing, where and to whom would I go? Faced with foreign ground, envisioning the worst possible outcome, I stood frozen until shaken by the sudden blast of the bell threatening my balance, even before I started.

The Meditation Center appeared over the hill. The narrow, winding road led to an old Benedictine monastery nestled in the forest. The sprawling brick building with its majestic, white columns had become the retreat center for Buddhist teachings. Metta, or loving- kindness, replaced Pax above the doorway. A lone stained-glass window remained to protect the basement on the far left of the building. It depicted Christ in the garden, which offered little consolation.

At twenty-six, I drove slowly toward the graveled driveway, sharply aware of each stone disturbed by the weight of the tires. The first uncertainty struck. Where do I park? This nearly paralyzed me. I prayed some fledgling like me would inquire so I could unwittingly follow suit, but there was no such miracle. A flat dirt area beyond the building with traces of trampled grass lay adjacent to the circular drive. It was then that I noticed a wooden brace with a placard attached: NO PARKING IN THE DRIVEWAY. Did that mean no stopping in the driveway? I would look foolish lugging all my stuff up this hill. Plagued by this dilemma, I decided looking foolish was better than the embarrassment of being told to move. While I had my fill of looking foolish, it was not nearly finished with me yet. Armed with pillows, blankets, sleeping bag, a very large suitcase, and a stash of food and caffeine, I felt duly protected by familiarity and control. I didn't even notice that *stuff* for the veteran meditators consisted of a sole parcel like a backpack slung over one shoulder. I proceeded to the appointed lot and dragged my stymied self up the hill. Several people were meandering as I made my way up the few cement steps that formed an apron around the oversized front door.

The vestibule was neatly lined with an array of footwear. I glanced about quickly, seeking direction, but found none. To my right, closed

French doors revealed a room with wall-to-wall bookcases. A large, red embroidered cloth hung above the fireplace. An eclectic group of old over-stuffed chairs circled the room. Taped to one of the small glass panes the sign read:

NO READING, EATING, or
NAPPING IN THE LIBRARY

How odd. "Does anyone know where you register for the retreat?" My booming voice cracked the pervasive silence and nearly derailed me. A tall, thin, bald figure in saffron robes—his dark, deep eyes avoiding my inquisitive gaze—gestured toward a framed entry into a large dining room. The odor of curried something assaulted my nostrils. I was grateful for the smuggled sustenance tucked in my suitcase. I made my way over to one of many long tables upon which several neatly stacked papers and a small metal box represented the only sign of activity. Silence prevailed.

The young woman seated at the table handed me two half sheets of paper without speaking or looking at me. Hmm. One read:

> While you are here you will refrain
> from: speaking any untruths; which
> means you will not speak.
> (or make eye contact by the way)
>
> you will not steal; which means
> you will not take anything that is not
> placed in your hand. *(huh?)*
>
> you will not kill any living
> being, including insects.
> *(but there are no screens and aren't
> we sleeping on the floor?)*
>
> you will not engage in sexual
> misconduct; which means you will
> not engage in sexual activity.
> *(no problem here)*

you will not take any
intoxicating substances which
includes caffeine.
(*I must have my coffee!*)

*Signed*_____

The other piece of paper read:
I will not hold The Center liable
should any misfortune occur while
I am here. (*that does it*)

Signed _____

A gasp stuck in my throat like a large piece of ice. The pen in my trembling fingers betrayed the dread that exploded my imagination. It was clear. This was unfamiliar territory, and I was not in control. My first instinct was to flee, but my discalced feet remained fixed to the chilly vinyl floor.

The blast of the morning bell must have mobilized my rigid body to the appropriate landing, because soon I was considering the danger in the slope back down with slightly more courage.

The gentle sound of the Tibetan bell resounded at perfect intervals. At the front of the meditation hall, the tall, thin man in orange appeared regal as he took his place on the cushion and read:

The Guest House

This being human is a guest house
Every morning a new arrival.
A joy, a depression, a meanness,
Some momentary awareness comes
As an unexpected visitor.
Welcome and entertain them all!
Even if they're a crowd of sorrows
Who violently sweep your house
Empty of its furniture.
Still treat each guest honorably.
He may be clearing you out
For some new delight.
The dark thought, the shame,
the malice, meet them at the door laughing,
And invite them in (for tea.)
Be grateful for whoever comes,
because each has been sent as a guide from beyond.[6]

I listened from the comfort of my zafu and realized that I had stayed for tea, grateful I didn't die.

Thus, the journey into Buddhism began. Sunanda, a young Christian woman from France, was the meditation teacher that weekend. This gentle woman, an act of surrender, and a "beginner's mind" taught me to meditate.[7]

I learned to watch as an imperceptible shadow standing just slightly behind the pain without being the pain, slightly behind the rage without becoming the rage, yet completely aware of it and nothing else. Learning to observe from slightly behind the thoughts, watching them come, letting them go, without dragging the nets, without changing a thing, without thrusting aside. Allowing it all to rise, have its presence acknowledged, without so much as a disturbance in the rhythm of the breath, before letting it go. Always, at every moment, at every hour, returning the attention to the place at the gate of the temple to simply watch, undisturbed. Just watch.

Chiang Tzu said, "The perfect man uses his mind as a mirror. It grasps nothing, it refuses nothing, it receives, but does not keep."[8]

If we meditate on the breath in and out, the rhythm of the universe is realized in the simple acceptance of gift and the task of letting go.

"If you do not come too close" you will recognize the palm of his hand.[9]

Prayer is too closely linked with the things that go on inside us and through the events of everyday life, remarks Hume. When we cannot focus on God, because "God cannot be known by thought; prayer becomes distasteful."[10] Thus, we are forced into just being and silence exposes the illusions we've held so dear.[11]

Dear Lord,

> *Beginning again, dancing about in the 'on- deck circle', it is with gratitude and love and "a heart held humble to level and light the way" that I return.*[12] *All points lead to the greater glory of God. Thank you.*

Lost

Standstill (instructed the Elder to children who may
become lost in the forest.)
The trees ahead and the bushes beside you are not lost.
Wherever you are is called here.
And you must treat it as a powerful stranger,
Must ask permission to know it and to be known.
The forest breathes. Listen. It answers. I have made this
place around you.
If you leave it, you may come back again, saying Here.
No two trees are the same to Raven. No two branches are
the same to Wren.
If what a tree or bush does is lost on you You are surely lost.
Standstill. The forest knows
Where you are, you must let it find you.[13]

CHOOSING

The Call

Samuel cried, "Here I am, Lord" (1Samuel 3:4). Abraham abandoned his homeland to sojourn in the wilderness (Genesis 21:34).

Moses fled into the desert, and we remain in awe. These biblical giants listened, heard, and responded (Exodus 2:15).

The call of God with-us prevails (Matthew 1:23).

The morning chill lingered. The bells resounded with an invitation to worship. They held no warning that a summons would supplant the habitual jaunt toward the vestibule with a piercing dread. As if struck by a bolt of lightning, I remained motionless upon the landing. *Am I being called to religious life?* The question so dominated the moment that it rendered all else impenetrable. Aware only of a fierce rebuttal forming in my pounding heart, I hadn't noticed the moist chill wrapped in wrenched palms lying stiffly at my side. Preposterous! I must have appeared visibly shaken but pretended to be simply preoccupied.

I was grateful for the lapse, which created some urgency as liturgy was about to begin. Comforted by the rhetoric, I successfully dismissed the proposal, but not the encounter.

Our lives are filled with endless crossroads. The choices we make both large and small have far-reaching effects, many of which we never truly grasp. "When the young man asked, 'what must I do to possess eternal life?' he went away sad because he couldn't make the total commitment, not because he didn't want to."[14]

It is rather our response "to the call and the question of God," said Bonhoeffer, "as opposed to the result of that call."[15]

The apostles responded by immediately abandoning their nets to follow him. The nets that we are asked to abandon are our work, our reluctance, our successes, and responsibilities. Not so immediately do we abandon these. We come more slowly. We so covet our time and talent. It is an extraordinary challenge to choose a spiritual life. In sophisticated and subtle ways, we often distance ourselves from God rather than deepen a relationship of intimacy. The closer we become to our own hearts and minds, the closer we come to God, then realize exactly what it is he is asking of us. He asks nothing less than to die with him, nothing less than to go beyond our limits, while resting in his promise of mercy and love.

Holiness is a "condition of complete simplicity costing not less than everything," says Eliot.[16]

Silesius once said, "God is the circle's center for those who dare embrace him. For those who merely stand in awe, he is the circle's rim."

Do we choose to stand in awe rather than embrace—dare to embrace—the living God? Does our life of prayer help us create the circle's rim[17] or become the circle's center?

"Being one with the universe, with our darkest enemy, and with God; that is what we wish for most, whether we know it or not," says Kunkel.[18]

Spiritual life is often described as a journey, a discovery of what it means to be human; the discovery of a "love great enough to bear the risk of both disclosure and discovery," says Merton.[19]

"It has not been primarily my seeking and searching that has been most important," says Muilenberg, "rather the awareness of being sought and found by another."[20]

Being found by the living God is about intention and grace, call and response, and presence.

Blessed are those who hunger and thirst for holiness, they shall be filled. (cf Matthew 5:6)

"Systems move in seemingly random, disorderly ways until it chooses a new direction at a higher level of expanded consciousness."

Are we but systems seeking a higher consciousness?[21]

After living in random disorder, the systems theory is hopeful, though the heart is not always. Fear though will often precede the knowing and knowing, once it occurs, is so much simpler than imagined, we barely notice without the drama.

Dear Lord,

> *May the grace of God and the assistance of his angels guide this journey. "Harden not my heart" (Psalm 95: 8), and help me to accept all things as part of a mystery greater than I could ever imagine. Help me to simply be still and listen. Amen.*

LONGING

Inside My Grandmother's Kitchen

The scent of lemon drifted in the air like fairy dust, nearly taking on the color of the tender veins of the freshly cut fruit from which the clear, spiced droplets were drizzled. A soft, dusted pouch of kneaded dough waited patiently on the table like a well-protected jewel transparently encased. A thin, cotton cloth, its faded blue stripes camouflaged by generous amounts of flour, draped over the mound.

Perched at the threshold, my excitement grew much larger than my tiny frame could hold. I made my way across the cracked, checkered brown tone linoleum of my grandmother's kitchen to the only empty seat at the table. Criss cross, criss cross. The soft mound was gathered from its place of honor to be deftly divided. Twin puffs were swiftly rolled and snaked across the surface. Twisting to form a perfect braid, they turned to meet, forming an equally perfect circle.

The bustle in the air might appear to the non-familial eye as chaotic. Everyone in the kitchen seemed to be speaking (loudly, at that), though not necessarily to one another. I recognized the order of things immediately, just as I had each year at Easter as far back as I could remember.

I took my place, kneeling on the red vinyl chair. Like being lifted onto familiar shoulders at a parade, my exposed bony knees recognized the cracks and creases with a tuft of graying stuffing always threatening to poke through. The frame, which extended around the chair like an all-encompassing hug, served as my protection from the large, soft bodies donning breast-covered aprons darting about the room. The chrome had long since lost its luster and decorative stones. Nonetheless, it proudly displayed years of wear from clinking together to fit yet another piece of furniture turned into a seat for another boisterous voice at the door. The 'barrel' was one such piece. Its service spanned two generations, at least! Looking more like a bongo drum with a padded top, it was small enough to tuck into the corner and large enough to hoist a small child to the table.

The sun-streaked room danced with anticipation as the creak from the oven door matched by a waving arm and the shout of "It's hot!" announced its unnecessary warning. The sound of the old chipped porcelain door was sufficient for even the smallest member in the room to halt until the warm waft of freshly baked bread diminished.

I slipped off the chair to see another creation safely deposited on the crowded rack. I weaved clumsily through the billows of cotton prints and stood in the doorway of one of the two bedrooms flanking the encompassing view from the oven door. I gazed at the makeshift clotheslines strung about the room, towering over the pure white sheets donning the wall-to-wall beds and oversized bureau. Countless strands of freshly made pasta lay carefully drying. My sisters and cousins darted among the cloaks, squealing with delight, and the chase was on. Suddenly a wisp of a floured mopine brushed my shoulder clearly in an effort to shoo the offenders from the sanctuary holding Sunday dinner. Innocuous threats of harm scattered the clan across the portal and out the door. I alone was left to witness the continuation of the litany of potential disasters.

It really didn't matter. We both knew I wasn't the guilty party. I never was. I inched my jolting legs back to my place of refuge. Instinctively, the nearest family member elevated me to safety, hesitating briefly in mid-air as my disobedient legs sought to coordinate in their place through the open back of the chair. My knees found the formed pouches they had previously occupied, warm and welcoming.

As the table was being transformed to prepare for the *past,* my eyes caught a glimpse of my sisters disappearing behind bare bushes. In the distance, the cadence echoed off the partially frozen ground amidst shrieks of joy. I proudly placed my neatly creased napkins and piles of freshly scratched cheese before me. Samples from the simmering pots aligned my works of art.

Eventually, I would come to embrace the inside looking out. Instead, I gripped the thickly buttered heel of fresh Italian bread as tenaciously as my *longing* to be pounding the unforgiving ground, and savored every morsel given for a job well done.

Psalm 63

O God you are my God—for you I long! For you my soul is thirsting.

My body pines for you like a dry weary land without water.

So, I gaze at you in the sanctuary to see your strength and your glory

For your love is better than life. My lips will speak your praise.

So, will I bless you all my life. In your name, I will lift up my hands.

My soul shall be filled as with a banquet. My mouth shall praise you with joy.

On my bed, I remember you. On you I muse through the night, for you have been my help, in the shadow of your wings

I rejoice, my soul clings to you. Your right hand holds me fast. (cf. Psalm 63)

O God,

How often have I begun to pray this Psalm and gotten no further than O God in either absolute awe or utter despair before the Blessed Sacrament or while pacing some parking lot? O God, how often have I neglected to recognize the gift of faith in simply being able to cry out, O God, much less *my God for whom I long*

He, who is the source and object of our longing! He, who calls us into being. He, the Alpha and the Omega, in the "summons and the sending," in my choosing and being chosen... for whom I long.[22]

For you my soul is thirsting.

"You will look for me, he says in John, where I am going you cannot come. I must leave you for a little while" (cf. John 7: 34–36). As he reveals and conceals himself in this lifelong mystery of divine hide and seek, the very thought, feeling, and image of him hides infinitely more.[23] Where what you do not know is all you know.[24] "As we learn to live with the restlessness of desire.[25] says St. Augustine

My body pines for you like a dry
weary land without water.

I was blessed with the experience of a dry, weary land, while hitchhiking across the desert in July. My daughter of three months and I were without food or water. All that I owned was in a broken-down car left behind. The temperature was 120° in the shade that day. I waited for the sun to set before proceeding across the hills to San Diego. It would have to be before dark as it might be snowing there. I rinsed out her pajamas with water from an old rusted faucet. I laid it on a large rock to dry. It was so hot that her last piece of protection against the elements literally caught fire!

"True love and prayer are learned in the moments when prayer becomes impossible and the heart has turned to stone," says Merton.[26]

I had $.35 in my pocket. "Freedom's just another word for nothing else to lose", sings Janis.[27] The sunset was as beautiful as I have ever seen that day.

So, I gaze on you in the sanctuary to see your strength and your glory.

I can wait, I can watch. I can listen, I can in all things prepare a place for you to come into my soul, but you alone will bring it to fulfillment, when you alone are all that I see.

"Something happens," says Rudolf Otto, in speaking of the experience of the "mysterium tremendum."[28] Something happens to the one who gazes on him in the sanctuary to see his strength and his glory. But no one is quite able to say what that something is.

Von Balthasar tries, "Quietly without our knowing it an angel comes and nudges us on the shoulder, the gate flies open, and we walk out past the sleeping guards to freedom."[29] Something happens without our knowing it and we are led to pray with conviction,

For your love is better than life.

Once there was a young monk in the forest monastery who went to the teacher and asked, "Master, I studied hard, learned all the sutras well, meditated diligently, and have been obedient in all things, but I long to know the truth. Please let me go to the mountain where I shall either die or find that which I seek. It does not matter, for I would rather die than live not knowing." Realizing that the young monk was prepared for such solitude, the master gave him the permission he sought. So, the young man packed up a few belongings tied onto the end of a stick over his shoulder and proceeded toward the mountain. As he was leaving the last village, he noticed an old man coming down. He thought, "Perhaps this old man knows something of which I seek. I will ask him, since it may be the last person I ever see." As he approached the old man, he told him the whole story of how hard he worked and how deeply he longed to see the truth, ending with, "Can you help me? Do you have any advice for me before I go?" (He did not realize, of course, that this was the famous Bodhisattva who appears to those ready for enlightenment.) The old man, who also carried his life's possessions upon his shoulder, looked at the young monk and—without a word— placed the bundle on the ground before him. In that moment, the young man leaped for joy! He understood in that simple act that the truth lies in the final letting go of all things. When he recovered from this magnificent experience, he said "Now what shall I do?" After all, he had this agenda prepared for the rest of his life. The old monk simply bent down and picked up his bundle and proceeded back to the marketplace.[30]

"You cannot know the truth, says Stephen Levine, you can only enter directly the moment in which truth resides."[31] To discover a love better than life, one must be prepared to die. Paul knew it. John Vianney knew it, too. "If only you knew how much God loves you, you would die for joy!"[32] He meant die!

"He who climbed the Mount of the Beatitudes, must necessarily climb the Mount of Calvary," says Sheen. "...to practice what he preached."[33]

> *My lips will speak your praise, so will I bless you all my life. In your name, I will lift up my hands. My soul shall be filled as with a banquet, my mouth shall praise you with joy! On my bed, I remember you...*

Metanoia has as much to do with remembering as longing. Emmanuel agrees. In answer to the question: How can there be such evil... so much injustice... how do we help?

"You can primarily begin by offering yourself another word, another definition for evil. When one says evil, whatever it is you are trying to do something about is immediately cast outside your heart, and outside your heart nothing can be done. Renamed more accurately, ask why is there so much forgetting in the world, so much unexpressed and unfulfilled longing. Verbalized that way the answer is clearer, is it not? What to do? To love, to love, to love. Become the loving teacher. Be who you are in as much love as you possess, as you have allowed yourself to remember. Be that loving, remembering human being within the company of the forgetter, and they will see your light when they are ready and they will hear you when they can and pray for them."[34]

> *On you I muse through the night, for*
> *you have been my help. In the shadow*
> *of your wings I rejoice. My soul clings*
> *to you; your right hand holds me fast.*

Sometimes when I muse through the night before drifting off to sleep, I pray a short form of compline or the ancient metta or loving-kindness meditation.

If there is anyone I have harmed this day, may I be forgiven *and to myself,* I forgive you.

If there is anyone who has hurt me, I forgive you.

May all beings, be peaceful.
May all beings be happy.
May all beings be strong in mind
and body.
May all beings know joy in the
acceptance of things just as they are.[35]

Now, master let your servant go in peace, according to your word, for my eyes have seen your salvation, which you prepared in the sight of all the peoples, a light of revelation to the gentiles and the glory for your people Israel."

(cf. Luke 2:29–32)

Glory be to the father and the son and the holy spirit, amen.

May the lord grant us a restful night, and a peaceful death, Amen.

Dear Jesus,

I love you from the fullness of a grateful heart bursting with joy. While still attempting to use words and "every attempt a different kind of failure," I surrender completely to you.[36] Now is the time. As a precious mosaic, you have pieced my life together. As a precious mosaic, you hold me in your hands. My responsibility is to gaze, only to gaze on the one for whom I live my life. Amen

LOVING

All Hallow's Eve

All Hallow's Eve of All Saints is the eve of All Souls. How convenient for the merciless sisters who reveled in enlightening little ones banished to released time the Tuesday before Halloween. What could be more disillusioning (or boring) than the theological exegesis exposing the origin of jack-o-lanterns and ghosts? It compares to none other than dispelling the myth of Santa Claus to a seven-year-old because "it's time." Time for what, no one can tell except by divine revelation, it's just one more of those obscurities, one more of life's cruelties. With any luck, some entrusted soul (no pun intended) would be complicit in sustaining the imagination for just a while longer.

In the meantime, the five Neri girls would impatiently hit the brisk air before dusk. Shuffling from house to house, the Windmill St. rounds took no less than three hours. Windmill Hill extended a mere half mile from ledge to end. Nearly everyone in the neighborhood was related to one another. I never quite got who was a *cumbard* and who was a *padine,* but I'm sure the translations were sufficiently broad to encompass almost anyone who spoke the same dialect, made home-made wine in the cellar, thought tomatoes, basil and garlic were staples and shared with anyone who happened by.

One such household at a time would complete the ritual of advancing the steamy masked horde of ghouls through the kitchen and past the plastic covered parlor in search of sufficient light. It was not until then that the query game could begin. Complete with "Oh mys" and "Aahs," there were always three guesses, and even though it was understood that the first two didn't count, we always pretended to be excited when our identity was finally revealed.

Since costumes were recycled amongst the clan each year, no contemplation was required, but what fun would that be? The threadbare legs approached the knees, the tattered tie had long since reached, and the sparkly stuff gave scarcely a hint of the proud skeleton it once had been. Yet, year after year, we donned our assigned character with glee. It wasn't until my elder sister elaborated on the gypsy costume she wore in "Fiddler on the Roof" that any of us realized that a costume did not have to come in a box.

There were few restrictions apart from being hit by a car. While costumes were economized, thankfully, candy bars were still whole and sampling was not only permissible, but unlimited. Nutrition and safety got very little press in those days. Paranoia had not permeated our *Leave it to Beaver* neighborhood. Fear of a razor blade showing up in an apple was still a few years off. There wasn't a presidential appointed committee to investigate childhood obesity, and no one ever heard of trans fat, much less knew what it was.

Despite the nuns, we lived in a sheltered era. Save the scarcity of means, we lived in an abundant time. Though secluded by culture and religion, the inherent kinship surpassed any hint of isolation. Thus, armed with *love,* the skeletons of yesteryear embrace the goblins of today and remember when.

"Expect everything, worry about nothing," says St Therese Lisieux. "Confidence and trust is a fundamental childhood attitude."[37]

It doesn't matter if we love God; the whole point is... God loves us. (cf 1 John 4: 10)

As children, we just knew that.

A woman struggling to be "good," but frustrated by her failure, asks Emmanuel, "How can I be more loving?" His reply, "You cannot instruct the heart to be loving. You can act loving, everyone can do that. But hearts do not open on command. You are commanding the child to behave and the child is attempting to behave. Rather, embrace yourself in your unlovingness and ask the child, why can you not love? Listen for the answer. You may be quite surprised at what you hear and gain a new respect for yourself. Moved to compassion for your own pain, you will then be more loving."[38]

To become more loving calls for a humble, listening heart which knows what it does not know and sees what is unknown. To become more loving calls us to stand still and ask permission to know the most universal, the most tremendous, the most mysterious of forces"[39]

To become more loving calls for forgetfulness of things created, remembrance of the Creator, and attention to that which is within.[40]

To become more loving calls us "to soar above transitory things, to be fond of solitude and silence, to be in the atmosphere of the Holy Spirit and respond with his inspirations.[41]

To become more loving calls us to not desire to do anything except that which is the will of God.

"Please call me by my true names so I can wake up", says Thich Nhat Hanh, "so the door of my heart can be left open, the door of compassion. "[42]

Dear Jesus,

It's New Years. A few candles, music, a loving-kindness meditation and we are like music not contained, bringing love without substance or form, bringing truth dancing before the world, pointing the way. This moment has come to matter more than what I will do with the rest of my life, because it is the rest of my life. My prayer, to do the father's will, to give him glory; that is all. Amen.

RECONCILING

I am stuck. I am stuck in a place between the mountain and the marketplace, in a place of sadness and regret. With e.e. cummings I had proclaimed, "the eyes of my eyes see, the ears of my ears awake."[43] Now, I can only speak from my disconnectedness. I was unable to live out that which I have been told.

It seems everything once uncovered has pride as its root. Most words only reflect the pride that supports the ego that refuses to give in. Self- forgetfulness turns out to be self-indulgence. Endurance to bear the relentless awareness of sinfulness becomes impossible. I am used up and worn out, and I can't say "I'm sorry" or "I love you" anymore. Besides, how can I still believe that what I say is true when experience tells me it isn't in the same moment?

"A clean heart, create for me, O God," I pray, "let me be like you in all my ways." (cf Psalm 51:10.) In all my ways, Lord? Why do I pray for such things when most times I'd rather pretend that I'm deaf, lower my eyes, and look away? If only I could remain steadfast.

What appears humble isn't, and transformation is a much different process than I had once supposed. It has become increasingly clear to me that with all that I am and am not there is no possible way that whatever good he manages through me could ever be anything but his care and his grace. As a matter-of-fact, I only seem to complicate and interfere with a very simple directive. Be one with him as he is with the father. It is for this that he has made me. This is the challenge. As he continues to call me, he continues to bless my soul.

God offers the promise of freedom from the imprisonment of our ego where misery and hope collide. Von Balthasar's account of just such a conflict is riveting:

"You lure me into a deadly adventure, saying you desire to comingle your breath with my very breathing. You are a beggar for love, but don't you see, we are made for measure and limits. You know nothing of measure, but I must maintain my boundaries and remember that you are God. When you threaten to grip my heart, if I say with all humility, "Lord go away from me, for I am a sinner," I can create distance. If I say, "I am not worthy that you should come under my roof, but leave the rest out," you will remain God. I will wash your feet, anoint your head, and adore you as when you were transfigured on the mountain, but please don't come down again. It is the religious thing to do, you know, to recognize the infinite, qualitative difference between God and the world".

By erecting a chapel somewhere in a snug corner, you will be preserved. I can visit you daily and pray the office.

"It will be a sign of my faith. I will stand before God eye to eye when your unfathomable glance pierces me. And I will long for wholeness. These are dangerous moments and times of anguish. But your gaze remains. Sometimes, if I pray very hard I can pray you away. Consumed by words, there's less chance of hearing you. Sooner or later, I will get the framework of my spirituality to replace you. And then, then I will have peace. It cannot be otherwise, you know; creatures have their measure and limits. And when this finitude encounters your infinite love, there is a fear of being burst asunder. It is a pious error to think we long for the infinite. Experience contradicts it. Instead we lay down our peace offering and ask that you be satisfied with it. Please don't trespass my boundaries. You may overwind the spring on the clock. Know that the measure by which I judge myself is a definite scale of perfection, which I have devised drawing on your clearly expressed prohibitions. I supplement those with voluntary works of love, so as not to hear your unclear and amorphous call to the undefined. My space is familiar to me, and only within can I know the world or even you. I do not long to go out of myself. By long association I have grown fond of this house of my suffering with all its shortcomings. I do not wish to be stripped down, but clothed over. You cannot exact the impossible feat that I should become a stranger to myself and at midnight like a thief climb out of my own window to a certain death."[44]

Please, please don't ask this of me.

T.S. Eliot describes the experience at the threshold of the unknown as being "in a dark wood on the edge of the grimpen menaced by monsters and fancy lights risking enchantment."[45]

The monsters and the enchantment are equally perilous. Perhaps the fancy lights are even more perilous. In either case it doesn't matter, because it will pass.

Jesus lifts us beyond our limited image of him again and again. We wait in a dark wood for his promise to return until he withdraws again that we might grow from impression to withholding to return in search of the inexhaustible mystery of God! That Tabor experience to which I held resolutely for far too long made it nearly impossible to continue in any direction.

Now, little by little, I yield to him, as little by little I see that his ways are not mine. I realize that I created an idol out of the image I fashioned for myself. This idol that I presumably melted and molded for him has not been his image at all. The likeness he offers me is that I may be who I am. In the journey toward wholeness, the very self I tried desperately to be rid of, has been, in fact, his highest gift to me.

The glory of God may be man fully alive, but the soul is afraid of dying and afraid of living in him at the same time. We are afraid to be with the one who has proven again and again to be all we need. The self hangs onto both the pain and the need! How silly we are in our stubbornness. It is a fight for survival. It won't give up easily. After all, this is the tangible proof that we exist, otherwise we are mere imagination, even less perhaps, and that scares me even more. The self continues to kick, holler, and scream. It will give up one day and, when it does, he will accompany me further into himself. Until then, I surrender and wait as I am able. That is all there is to do.

Thus, I found the courage to pray with Carlo Carretto,

> "Come then, death, come. I am waiting. You do not frighten me anymore; I no longer see you as a foe. I see you as my sister. I look you in the face. I understand you now. As

you come towards me I tell you, held firm in your mighty hand, do with me as you will. Wholeheartedly, I say this to you, truthfully, I say this to you, lovingly I say this to you, do with me as you will. Accustom me to this extreme abandonment. Accustom me to this never ending adult kiss, to this never finished conversation. Accustom me little by little, by distributing my death through all the days of my life. Put it on my bread like ashes or sand that I may not live by bread alone. Put it in my house as something lacking, that I may never accept the limitations of the visible. Put it as insecurity in my security, that I may only be secure in him alone. Put it in the midst of my joy as a reminder, so that I may become used to being alone for that moment when I shall be alone with you."[46]

But God defies containment and the "hour" of my tryst with "death" had not come. My beckoning to go beyond my "measure and limits" simply rendered me helpless and oppressed. That which restrained me, plagued me. I realized later that passion leads to intimacy, then to fear of pain, and finally to fear of being utterly alone

I pleaded for peace, or rather for relief. "But then you would not know true joy," he replied.

"You will know very little until you get there. You will journey blind, but this way leads toward possession of what you have sought for in the wrong place. What do you know of the kind of suffering you must undergo on the way?"[47]

I met with my meditation teacher today. "I'm frightened," I said. "There's nothing left to hold on to. So much is illusion." "Can you gently let go of what you leave behind while embracing what lies before you?" he said. He captured the posture which nearly destroyed me. I was pushing away, while protecting against. Such clarity! Thank you.

"All things good and bad come and go," my grandmother used to say in Italian.

Suffering is wishing it were otherwise.

Dear Lord,

> *I find myself holding the breath of my thoughts, knowing you will bring to completion the good you have begun, knowing my heart, my mind, and my understanding are much too small. I know too that in a moment I will question and complicate the very word I hold this moment to be my reason for being. For so long, I have trembled on a distant shore, gazing into the abyss which separates us; for all too long. Eternal is your mercy from age to age. Lamb of God, you take away the sins of the world, speak but the word, and my soul shall be healed. Amen*

AWAKENING

"Eyes Have Not Seen and Ears Have Not Heard"
(cf. 1Corinthians 2:9)

The air was warm and sticky. I noticed a faint mist rising just above the irregular surface from where I lay on the stony asphalt. There was a piercing pain at the back of my head; whether it was mist or blood that moistened the nape of my neck was difficult to distinguish. My focus was rather fixed on the paralyzing glare of the oncoming headlights directly in front of me. Time as I knew it stood still. I became absorbed in one interminable moment when that which appeared inevitable seemed strangely okay. It's never been clear to me what happened next. The luminous, concentric beams merged until the muddied pieces of splintered treads etched its tracks in my memory forever.

It was the sting of tears washing over minor cuts and bruises on my face that awakened me. I was lying on a hard, paper-covered table alone, filled with questions and confusion. What happened? How did I get here? Aloof and preoccupied, the occasional health care worker who entered the room was less than interested in my mysterious arrival. I could only recall the brush of air disturbed by whirling treads.

This experience was easier to forget than grasp until some years later when I found myself on a cold steel table consumed by pain and fear. A crowd of health care providers anxiously hovered while inquiries flew. "Where's the father? Who will decide between baby and mother?"

"He isn't here," I retorted, surprised the lucidity of my voice went unnoticed.

"Save my baby, of course!" Why in the world would that even be a question? Why was everyone so frantic? More importantly, why weren't they listening? Suddenly, I was struck by a shattering clarity. Instruments clanged with incisive tones. My vantage point changed indiscernibly to the far right corner of the room. There "I" was looming above the clamor. Any effort to comfort the crowd, who by this time were blaming each other for my loss, was futile. "It's okay, really. It's okay. It's no one's fault," but my pleading fell on deaf ears.

The group below began focusing on the remaining life, desperate not to feel liable for two lives in one day. Then, my attention was drawn as if by a powerful magnet to a light, more by its brightness than its glare. I felt stilled more than paralyzed, by a penetrating sense of familiarity, oddly like returning home. The light, the stillness, the gaze united, whether it was a voice or a thought was not clear. I only know that I was offered a choice. Did I want to go home (toward the light) or go back? Instantaneously, "Home, of course," diffused immeasurable space followed just as quickly by a less penetrating whisper. "But who will care for my baby?" My attention had turned to the lifeless form below. Torn by that which was beyond comprehension and my responsibility to this child seemed to be the answer in itself. The decision was made. What happened next is less intelligible. The room was quieter now. I heard Apgar three, a faint cry, then nothing until I awoke two days later grasping cold metal rails alone.

While language often betrays the inexplicable, I submit to the poets and prophets who have mastered profound simplicity.

> "We are placed in this world for a little while that we might learn to bear the beams of love." Wm. Blake[48]

That which has been written again and again for our deaf ears to hear, placed before us again and again for our blind eyes to see has tugged at our hearts for years only to be qualified and rejected. How can one ever reproduce in pictures, sound or word the love this God holds in his heart for each of us? I think my heart will break. Life, though, is filled with "ten thousand joys and ten thousand sorrows;" from Tabor to Calvary and back to resurrection.[49] After the plunge into his loving hands, which we cannot begin to understand, after the struggle to hang onto who knows what, when there is no further violence to fear because death itself "has dealt its fiercest blow and lost," he comes.[50] "As a small, still voice," he comes (1 Kings 19:12). Without words, we reach to touch his garment. Without words, he heals our wounds. In fear and disbelief, we tremble to realize that he truly is the Son of God. It is not coincidental that I now have no energy of my own to alter this course. All that has come before is meaningless. All that I learned in years previous largely wasted. I surrender because there is nothing left to do. It bears no affirmation, I assure you. I let it be with complete abandon. I allowed my spirit to be surrounded by the God of hosts who, in his everlasting mercy, gives me his grace and his love. His grace and love is all I need. What happens next? I don't know.

What's different? Everything. What do I think about all this? Absolutely nothing. What do I discern from all this? There is nothing in the world of which he is not a part, absolutely nothing.

Lift, place, step. I made my way to the front of the meditation hall where the altar, adorned with flowers from the gardens surrounding the monastery, held a beautifully carved statue of Buddha. I was still wrapped in a thin, soft shawl, but it provided little comfort. A solid, heavy presence in the center of my chest prevailed—obscure yet inescapable. I made my way across the main dining room. Seeking solace, I ascended the stairs leading through the annex to my enclosure with this nebulous mass rising and falling with each passing breath. Step, step, intention, reach; the thud of the door echoed softly through the vacant corridor.

As if the final inaudible click of the door handle was itself permission, this pain became more discernable and demanded my attention. I sat at the edge of the simple wooden bed frame and leaned forward in anguish. I began to sob. Time was measured in moments. A cushion had been created by my arms folded tightly across my chest as the assault danced about. My tears bathed the small hairs on my arms before falling onto my lap which had steadied itself with the gentleness of a begging bowl. I cannot recall a more penetrating *scream!* I cannot imagine surviving greater intensity than this; all in deafening silence. Oddly, unfamiliar faces began to stream before me in an endless parade. It was incomprehensible and irrational.

Eventually, the gasp that had paralyzed me, released me. As I turned, I was struck by three trees framed by the open window. One was young and tender, one lay partially decayed on the forest floor, the other stood tall.

Yes, death is not personal. It just is. Everything lives and everything dies. It is a matter of course.

Later, a small group purported to be experienced meditators gathered in guru alley for an assigned check-in with the teacher. Each made their way into the room seeking either the most or the least comfortable space which was sure to disturb the depth of samahdi or concentration which had accumulated in days previous. I have never quite understood why this group is distinguished from the beginners, but then I have never been a fan of group meetings.

Nevertheless, it was my turn, so I recounted the experience briefly and asked, "What was that?" I was certain that somewhere in the volumes of Buddhist psychology and meditation there was a simple explanation for this clearly confounding experience that still vibrated within me. "I don't know," he replied. I cannot recall the speculation that followed. In the recounting, I had already betrayed the actual experience, which, in itself, was answer enough.

What was that? I had asked. The journey toward selflessness has been a difficult and dangerous one. Whether it is to the Buddhist void or the self-forgotten toward self-annihilation or union with the living God. Labels are meaningless. The self that I thought I knew no longer exists. Nothing is familiar.

"I peered into the water today; no one was there," I wrote. What I did not write was, "fear was conspicuously absent."

A rambling disjointed entry followed:

The ego deflates like a pin in a hot air balloon, but not before its time.

Grace is ever-present We are simply human, simply human no more, no less, divine only in him, drowned in sorrow, can't go back, this breath please. He has died, once for all that we might live!

This moment please, except seductive and cunning, feelings of accomplishment got caught in the net, a job well done for clocking hours on a zafu. As if one can step into a moment having shed its ego. The experience was less a breakthrough, even though something did shift within me, which was also seductive; it was just... pride. It was just one more construct in a yet to be revealed infinite layer of defense, disguising pride. What you think is, often isn't, and as Eliot says, "the only wisdom to acquire is humility and humility is endless."[51]

In a moment that too was gone.

I recall what I learned early on, watch your thoughts, at every moment, at every hour, simply watch. Let them go, without dragging the nets, without changing a thing, without thrusting aside. Allow it all to rise and fall. I recall Carretto, "Accustom me little by little, by distributing my death through all the days of my life."[52]

There is no prescription leading to this place and no prescription leading from it.[53] Selflessness is not the desire to not be, says Roberts. "That which is annihilated is the knowing of the thought and feeling of self not in God." "... from the fullness of a grateful heart, he rejoices that he is and at the same time desires unceasingly to be freed from the knowing and feeling of this being?."[54]

This place, which I feared for so long, this oneness within and without at the same time, for which I have no frame of reference, unspectacular and impermanent, in moment to moment, either self-fulfilled or self-less, the living God continues to teach my soul. So, after years of an inward movement, I began years of an outward movement, at peace with this prayer:

"luminous tendril of celestial wish... through twilight's mystery made flesh... teach disappearing also me the keen illimitable secret of begin."

—e.e. cummings[55]

Dear Jesus,

It has been a day marked by loose ends and blessings. Grace lifts my eyes to you; I hear you in the breath of life around me. As bread blessed and broken, we recognize you, as from dream through deception, what's possible emerges.

"I am who am." You are, we are empty vessels, channels of your love. (Exodus 3:14). You are the potter, we the clay, (cf Isaiah 64:7) into being from the stillness, we now pray "my soul does proclaim the greatness of the Lord; my spirit rejoices in you" (Luke1:46), God my Savior. Amen

One day, while attempting to meditate, I encountered a spider on the nearby radiator. The spider was more interesting than the metta phrases this sitting, so I stopped and watched as the frenetic pace became an attempt to climb. "May you be safe and protected" I continued the blessings, "May you find peace in acceptance of just who you are." Metta came easily for this creature. No surprise. Nature has been my anchor since the start. He kept trying to climb, falling to safety shortly thereafter again and again. He reached millimeter heights over previous efforts, which sounds a lot like my practice.

My joyful interest intensified and then it happened. He climbed ever so far up the wall to where and why I did not know, I only felt his steadfastness with such compassion. Ugh! He fell. My heart fell with him. What a disappointment. I wanted him to succeed because that is what he seemed to want. I rooted for him: "You can do it, come on, you can do it." But he couldn't do it. He fell, not physically hurt, but he did not try again. He came to the end of the heater and disappeared. A lifetime changes in the walk from here to there; then it is gone. I felt a certain emptiness and a certain familiarity. Equanimity comes in the acceptance (and letting go) of things just as they are one moment at a time.

Joseph leaned forward from his place at the front of the meditation hall and smiled. "I am going to tell you the secret of Nirvana!" he said. "Ready?

"There is no separateness."

He paused then asked, "Did anyone get enlightened?" A murmur of laughter swept across the meditation hall. "Well then," he said, settling back onto his cushion in his forever perfect pose, "shall we meditate?"

Thirty years later and the driveway is neatly paved now. The austerity of a thin slab of foam for a bed has been replaced through the generosity of benefactors with simply furnished cells. The aroma of delicious vegetarian cooking replaces the pungent smell of unfamiliar spices from a far-off land.

After all, this is not a forest monastery in Burma. I never trekked thousands of miles across rough terrain to join courageous seekers from the West. Nor have I fallen ill from disease, mosquitos, or unclean water. As it turns out, it is not the necessary evil I once thought it was. A moment here, a moment there, West or East, is still just a moment; nothing to earn. The truth prevails in the acceptance of gift and the task of letting go; or rather *be,* says Jon Kabat-Zinn.[56] With this in-breath and this out-breath, the hunter becomes the warrior, and the warrior discovers all in all. No big deal.

> "With this he closed his eyes to descend into darkness, and when he opened them the separation had been removed. It was the world which had always existed in his heart but which only begins to beat the moment one beats in union with it," says Auguste, in *Smile at the Foot of the Ladder.*[57]

While it is an impossible task, I will attempt to relate an experience of oneness. Yes, we are connected—letters on paper to make words non- describable of the fact that one is in all and all is in one. The trees ahead and the creatures beneath them know much more than I of the immensity of the cosmos to which we belong.

More than thirty years have passed. It is still one sitting at a time, one step in the forest. This step.. when a moment explodes revealing the universe in a single "grain of sand... a flower,"[58] it's true. The trees find you if you... let them. That is also true. The ache in my left knee pulsates, comes, goes, and comes again like a warm blanket this time, as the lawnmower hums across the lawn like a badly tuned organ unable to drown out the bellows of the birds from the nearby trees through the dance of the breeze off my cheek, one moment, no matter, no difference., just is.

"A million ages in the past before the world had yet begun I danced in the garden all alone and I and me were one. The years have come, the years have gone with much to know and do, the garden gate is closed to us while I and me are two. The garden walls are crumbling now as do gives way to be and Yahweh reaches to enfold as I blend into me."[59]

How could one ever hope to express the gratitude owed to countless persons who bring us such teachings; Buddhist or Christian. We are all "enlightened". We have always known that. Each moment offers the opportunity to step into now; shed the confines of our narrow sense of self, and experience the love which holds all beings together around this container, his vessel, emptied and receptive to be his conduit in the world. All prayer, all action, all thought, either contributes to the force of nature or destroys it. The onus of the responsibility lies in the practice of the presence of this moment we call now.

May all beings be safe and protected. May all beings be peaceful.

May all beings be strong in mind and body.

May all beings share in the joy of acceptance of things just as they are.

A Rabbi spent years in solitude meditating on the mystery of the divine in all things a feeble approximation of what he had discovered was written in books. He later remarked, "I had hoped to help but perhaps I should not have spoken at all."[60]

The End

ENDNOTES

[1] John W. De Gruchy, Confessions of a Christian Humanist (Fortress Press, 2006), 22.

[2] St. John of the Cross and Kathleen Jones, The Poems of St. John of the Cross (New York: Burns and Oates, 2001), 12.

[3] H.vander Looy, Rule for a New Brother (Springfield Illinois: Templegate Publishers, 1976), 63.

[4] Ambrose of Milan, Seven Exegetical Works. (Catholic University of America,)

[5] Carlos Casteneda, A Separate Reality: Further Conversations with Don Juan (New York: Pocket Books, 1971) 85.

Beginning

6   Coleman Barks, trans .,The Essential Rumi (New York: Harper One, 1995), 109.

7   Shunry Suzuki, Trudy Dixon ed., Zen Mind, Beginner's Mind (Boston, Massachusetts: Weatherhill Publications, 1974), 1.

8   Frederick Franck, trans., Chuang Tzu, The Book of Angelus Silesius (Santa Fe, New Mexico: Bear and Co., Inc.),101.

9   T.S. Eliot, The Complete Poems, 1909–1950 (Orlando, Florida: Harcourt Brace and Co., 1980), 123.

10   Johnston, W. ed. The cloud of unknowing and The book of privy counselling (New York: Image Books, 1973)

11   Cardinal Basil Hume O.S.B., Searching for God (New York: Ampleforth Abbey Press, 2002),? 38

12   Elizabeth Roberts and Elias Amidon ed., 365 Prayers, Blessings and Life Prayers from Around the World (San Fran- cisco: Tree Claude Book, Harper, 1996), 70.

13   David Wagoner, Lost: The Best American Poetry (New York: Pemalink, 1999)

Choosing

[14] Cardinal Basil Hume O.S.B., Searching for God (New York: Ampleforth Abbey Press, 2002), 153.

[15] Dietrich BonHoeffer, Geffrey B. Kelly and John D. Godsey, Discipleship (Minneapolis, MN., First Fortress Press, 2003), 74.

[16] T.S. Eliot, The Collected Poems 1909 -1950, 209.

[17] Frederick Franck, trans., Chuang Tzu, The Book of Angelus Silesius (Santa Fe, New Mexico: Bear and Co., Inc.),101.

[18] Dorothy Berkley Phillips, The Choice is Always Ours: The Classic Anthology on the Spiritual Way (Wheaton, Il.: Theosophical Publishing House, 1974), 10.

[19] Thomas Merton, Contemplative Prayer (New York: Image Books, 1996), 14.

[20] The Choice is Always Ours, 36.

[21] Ann Marriner-Tomey and Martha Raile Alligood, Nursing Theorists and their Work, Health as Expanding Conscious-ness by Margaret A. Newman R.N. PhD. (Philadelphia, Pennsylvania: Mosby, 2006), 499.

LONGING

22   Donald J. Moore, Martin Buber: Prophet of Religious Secularism: The Criticism of Institutional Religion in the Writings of Martin Buber (Philadelphia: Jewish Publication Society of America, 1974), 131.

23   Jonathon Kirsch, Moses: A Life (New York: Ballantine Books, 1999), 115.

24   T.S. Eliot, The Complete Poems and Plays; 1909–1950 (Orlando, Florida: Harcourt Brace and Co., 1980), 126

25   Augustine, Confessions, trans. Henry Chadwick (Oxford: Oxford University Press, 1991), 29–30 (11.10)

26   Thomas Merton, Contemplative Prayer (New York: Image Books, 1996), 14.

27   Malcolm R. Westcott, The Psychology of Human Freedom: A Human Science Perspective and Critique (University of Michigan: Spring-Verlag, 1988), 199.

28   Rudolf Otto and John W. Harvey, The Idea of the Holy; An Inquiry into the Non-Rational Factor in the Idea of the Divine and its Relation to the Rational (Whitefish, Mont., Kessinger reprints, 2005),12.

29   Hans Urs von Balthasar, Heart of the World (San Francisco: Liturgical Press, 1979), 144.

30   Jack Kornfield, A Path with Heart: A Guide Through the Perils and Promises of the Spiritual Life (New York: Bantam Books, 1993), 154.

31   Stephen Levine, A Gradual Awakening (New York: Anchor Books, 1989.) 75.

32   J. Donald Walters, Promise of Immortality; The True Teaching of the Bible and the Bhagavad Gita (New Delhi: Sterling Publishers, 2003), 70.

33   Fulton Sheen, Life of Christ (New York: Sheed and Ward, 1958), 145.

34   Pat Rodegast and Judith Stanton, Emmanuel's Book: A Manual for Living Comfortably in the Cosmos (New York: Bantam Books, 1987), 47.

35   Sharon Salzberg, The Revolutionary Art of Happiness (Boston, Massachusetts: Shambhala Publications, 1995), 37.

36   T.S.Eliot, The Complete Poems, 1909–1950 (Orlando, Flor- ida: Harcourt Brace and Co., 1980), 182.

LOVING

[37] Gordon S. Wakefield, ed. Westminster Dictionary of Christian Spirituality (Philadelphia, PA.: Westminster Press, 1983), 377.

[38] Valerie Mylonas and Clifford Pia, a film, A Meeting with Emmanuel (Westport Connecticut: Friends Productions, 1990)

[39] Ursula King, The Spirit of One Earth: Reflections on Teilhard de Chardin and Global Spirituality (University of Michigan: Paragon House, 1989), 179.

[40] St. John of the Cross and Edgar Allison Peers, Spiritual Canticle and Poems (London: Burns and Oates, 1978), 470.

[41] Thomas Merton, Counsels of Light and Love of St. John of the Cross (New York: Burns and Oates, 2007) 63.

[42] Thich Nhat Hanh, The Collected Poems of Thich Nhat Hanh (Berkeley: Parallax Press, 1999), 73.

Reconciling

[43] Edward Estlin Cummings, 100 Poems (New York: Grove Press, 1954)

[44] Hans Urs von Balthasar, Heart of the World, 121

[45] T.S. Eliot, The Complete Poems, 1909–1950, 125–126.

[46] Carlo Carretto, Letters from the Desert (Maryknoll, New York: Orbis, 1972), 120.

[47] T.S. Eliot, The Complete Poems, The Cocktail Party, 146–147

Awakening

[48] Alfred Kazin,ed., The Portable Blake (New York: Penguin, 1976), 86.

[49] Jack Kornfield, After the Ecstasy, The Laundry: How the Heart Grows Wise on the Spiritual Path (New York: Bantam Books, 2000), 312.

[50] Homer, trans. from the Greek by Alexander Pope esq., The Iliad (Edinburgh,1769), 70.

[51] T.S.Eliot, Four Quarters, East Coker, 1940, 2

52 Carlo Carretto, Letters from the Desert Maryknoll, New York: Orbis, 1972, 120.

53 Thomas Merton, Choosing to Love the World: On Contemplation (Boulder, Colorado: Sounds True Inc., 2008), 35.

54 Bernadette Roberts, The Path to No-Self: Life at the Center (Albany: State University of New York Press, 1991), 141.

55 Edward Estlin Cummings, 100 Poems (New York: Grove Press, 1954), 119.

56 Jon Kabat-Zinn Ph.D., Full Catastrophe Living: Using the Wisdom of Your Body and Mind to Face Stress, Pain, and Illness (New York: Delta Press, 1990)

57 Henry Miller, Smile at the Foot of the Ladder (New York: New Directions, 1974), 39.

58 David V. Erdman ed., The Complete Poetry and Prose of William Blake: Auguries of Innocence (New York: Anchor Books, 1988), 490.

59 Anonymous

60 Jack Kornfield and Christina Feldman ed.., Soul Food: Stories to Nourish the Spirit and the Heart (New York: Harper Colllins Publishers, 1996), 232.

WORKS CITED

Adams, William Davenport. William Davenport Adams Papers, 1882-1904. New Jersey, Princeton University Library, 1882.

Ambrose, of Milan. Seven Exegetical Works. Washington [D.C.], Catholic University of America Press in association with Consortium Press, 2010.

Augustine, Saint. Confessions. Translated by Henry Chadwick, Oxford, Oxford

University Press, 1991.

Balthasar, Hans Urs von. Heart of the World. San Francisco, Liturgical Press, 1979.

Banks, Coleman. The Essential Rumi'. New York, Harper One, 1995.

Barclay, William. The Gospel of Matthew. Volume 2. Louisville, Ky, Westminster John Knox Press, 2001.

Blake, William. The Complete Poetry and Prose of William Blake: Auguries of Innocence. Edited by David V. Erdman, New York, Anchor Books, 1982.

Blake, William, and Alfred Kazin. Portable Blake. Markham, On, Penguin Books Canada, 1977.

Bon Hoeffer, Dietrich, et al. Discipleship. Minneapolis, MN, First Fortress Press, 2003.

Carretto, Carlo, and Rosemary Hancock. Letters from the Desert. Maryknoll, N.Y., London, Orbis Books; Darton, Longman and Todd, 2012.

Casteneda, Carlos. A Separate Reality: Further Conversations with Don Juan. New

York, Pocket Books, 1971.

Cummings, E E. 100 Selected Poems. Franklin Classics, 2018.

Dawson, J L, et al. A Concordance to the Complete Poems and Plays of T.S. Eliot.

Ithaca, Cornell University Press, 1995.

De Grunchy, John W. Confessions of a Christian Humanist. Fortress Press, 2006.

Eliot, T S. Complete Poems and Plays: 1909-1950. Boston, Mass, Houghton Mifflin Harcourt, 2014.

Emmanuel, Spirit, et al. Emmanuel's Book: A Manual for Living Comfortably in the Cosmos. Toronto; New York, Bantam Books, 1987.

Feick, Gertrude. Cardinal Basil Hume: A Pilgrim's Search for God. Leominster, Herefordshire, United Kingdom, Gracewing, 2019.

Hall, Gary P. Autonomy and Surrender; Solitude and Intimacy.

thomasmertonsociety.org, 2 Nov. 2009.

Hanh, Thich Nhat. Call Me by My True Names: The Collected Poems. Parallax Press, 1999.

Hardy, Alister-Claverina (Sir). The Spiritual Nature of Man; a Study of Contemporary Religious Experience. California, Clarendon Press, 1979.

Homer, and Alexander Pope. The Iliad of Homer. Baltimore, F Lucas, and N.G. Maxwell, 1819.

Hume, Basil. In Praise of Benedict, 480-1980 A.D. Petersham, Mass., St. Bede's Publications, 1994.

---. Searching for God. London, Hodder and Stoughton, 1979.

Jones, Kathleen. The Poems of St. John of the Cross. New York, Burns and Oates, 2001.

Kabat-Zinn, Jon. Full Catastrophe Living: Using the Wisdom of Your Body and Mind to Face Stress, Pain, and Illness. 1990. New York, Bantam Books, 2013.

King, Ursula. The Spirit of One Earth: Reflections on Teilhard de Chardin and Global

Spirituality. New York, Paragon House, 1989.

Kirsch, Jonathon. Moses: A Life. New York, Ballantine Books, 1999.

Kornfield, Jack. A Path with Heart. [S.I.], Random House Publishing Group, 2009.

---. After the Ecstasy, the Laundry: How the Heart Grows Wise on the Spiritual Path.

New York, Bantam Books, 2001.

---. Dharma Talk. Meditation Retreat, Dec. 1981.

---. The Wise Heart: A Guide to the Universal Teachings of Buddhist Psychology. New York, Bantam Books, 2009.

Kornfield, Jack, and Christina Feldman. Soul Food: Stories to Nourish the Spirit and the Heart. San Francisco, Harpersanfrancisco, 1996.

Lange, Johann Peter, and Philip Schaff. A Commentary on the Holy Scriptures. New York, C. Scribner's Sons, 1877.

Levine, Stephen. A Gradual Awakening. New York, Anchor Books, 1989.

Lewis, C S, and Clyde S Kilby. A Mind Awake: An Anthology of C.S. Lewis. San Diego, Harcourt Brace, 1968.

Lewis, C.S. The Four Loves. New York, Harcourt Books, 1968.

Lockman. New American Standard Bible: Text Edition. Anaheim, California, Foundation Publications, 1997.

Merton, Thomas. Contemplative Prayer. New York, Image, 1996.

- --. Counsels of Light and Love of St. John of the Cross. Mahwah, N.J., Hiddenspring, 2007.

- --. Thoughts in Solitude. New York, Farrar, Straus, Giroux, 2000.

Merton, Thomas, and M Basil Pennington. Thomas Merton: I Have Seen What I Was

Looking for: Selected Spiritual Writings. Hyde Park, NY, New City Press, 2005.

Merton, Thomas, and Jonathan Montaldo. Choosing to Love the World: On Contemplation. Boulder, Colo., Sounds True, 2015.

Miller, Henry, et al. The Smile at the Foot of the Ladder. San Francisco, The Greenwood Press, 1955.

Moore, Donald J. Martin Buber: Prophet of Religious Secularism: The Criticism of Institutional Religion in the Writings of Martin Buber. Philadelphia, Pennsylvania, Jewish Publication Society Of America, 1974.

Mylonas, Valerie, and Pia Clifford. A Meeting with Emmanuel; a Film. Westport, Connecticut, Friends Productions, 1990.

Newman PhD., Margaret A., et al. Nursing Theorists and Their Work, Health as Expanding Consciousness. Philadelphia, Pennsylvania, Mosby, 2006.

Otto, Rudolf, and John W Harvey. The Idea of the Holy: An Inquiry into the Non-Rational Factor in the Idea of the Divine and Its Relation to the Rational. London Alpha Edition, 2020.

Peers, Edgar Allison. St. John of the Cross, Spiritual Canticle and Poems. London, Burns and Oates, 1978.

Phillips, Dorothy Berkley, et al. The Choice Is Always Ours: The Classic Anthology on the Spiritual Way. San

Francisco, Calif., Guild for Psychological Studies Pub. House, 2004.

Randall, Diane C. She of the Dreaming Sky. Atlanta, GA, Pearl's Book'em Publisher, 2005.

Roberts, Bernadette. The Path to No-Self: Life at the Center. Albany, N.Y., State

University of New York Press, 1991.

Roberts, Elizabeth, and Elias Amidon. Life Prayers from around the World 365 Prayers, Blessings and Affirmations to Celebrate the Human Journey. New York, New York, Harper Collins Publishers Inc., 1996.

Russell, Bertrand. History of Western Philosophy. Bulwell Lane, Basford, Bertrand Russell Peace Foundation, 1996.

Ryan, Thomas. Prayer of Heart and Body: Meditation and Yoga as Christian Spiritual Practice. New York, Paulist Press, 1995.

Salzberg, Sharon. The Revolutionary Art of Happiness. Boston, Mass., Shambhala, 1995.

Sheen, Fulton J. Life of Christ. New York, Sheed and Ward, 1958.

Shunryu Suzuki, and Trudy Dixon. Zen Mind, Beginner's Mind: Informal Talks on Zen Meditation and Practice. New York, Weatherhill, 1974.

Silesius, Angelus. The Book of Angelus Silesius. Translated by Frederick Franck, Santa Fe, New Mexico, Bear and Co., Inc., 1985.

The Cloud of Unknowing: And the Book of Privy Counseling. Edited by W. Johnston, The Doubleday Religious Publishing Group, 1973.

"The Real Meaning of Life and Human Existence." New Age Spirituality, Alba Dase LLC, 2004, www.new-agespirituality.com. Accessed 6 Oct. 2009.

Tozer, A.W. The Pursuit of God; Finding the Divine in the Everyday. Peabody, MA, Christian Publications, 1993.

van der Looy, H. Rule for a New Brother. Springfield, Illinois, Templegate Publishers, 1976.

Wakefield, Gordon S. The Westminster Dictionary of Christian Spirituality. Philadelphia, Westminster Press, 1983.

Walters, Donald J. The Promise of Immortality; the True Teaching of the Bible and the Bhagavad Gita. New Delhi, Sterling Publishers, 2003.

Westcott, Malcolm R. The Psychology of Human Freedom: A Human Science Perspective and Critique. New York, Springer, 1988.